Breaking a Mare

Christina Thatcher grew up between a farm and a ranch house in Bucks County, Pennsylvania. She won a Marshall Scholarship to study in the UK and now lectures at Cardiff University. Her poetry and short stories have been widely published in literary magazines, including *Ambit, Poetry Wales, The North* and *The Poetry Review*. She has published two earlier collections, *More than you were* and *How to Carry Fire*. Christina has toured internationally, reading her work in the UK, USA, Canada, Costa Rica, Switzerland and Romania. She lives with her gardener husband, Rich, and their cat, Miso.

christinathatcher.com

@writetoempower

Praise for *Breaking a Mare*:

'What a precision feat this book pulls off. On the one hand, these are poems of sleek physicality – of clasp and bit and buckle and braid – with shrewd things to say about the tyranny of polish and perfection. At the same time, they're intimately attuned to the charged spaces we occupy and the roles we perform within them, whether it be a rodeo arena, a haunted hayride, a school playground or an empty kitchen. The result is a collection that closes the distance between the rodeo and the home, between the knacker man and the childhood game, between the trick rider and the teenager learning the use of discipline: the voices here know that one as much as the other contains the threat of harm and the conditions for joy. *Remember, girl, this is about control*, says one of the voices, and it could be a wink from the poet herself: savvy, heedful, scrupulously threading her way through danger, making it all look effortless. I am, like one of her riders, *lovestruck quick for all of it*.' – **Abigail Parry**

'*Breaking a Mare* is a magnificent exploration of female physicality, domination, and resistance. At its heart is the sacred relationship between human and horse, girl-woman and mare – a profound metaphor for the complex dynamic between a mother both breaking *and* empowering a daughter. With command and precision, Christina Thatcher has worked poems into being that are tightly wrought, each braided to the next. The skilful use of space and form gifts the reader another level of physical interaction, and such is the quality of the language that these poems give physical pleasure when read aloud. This is a book of real muscle. The poems are alive, rearing up, inviting us to ride our hurts and sorrows to find our strong and our *soft*. Christina Thatcher is an exceptional writer, a poet who refuses to *stay quiet*. Her speaker has galloped *out of darkness*, urging us now to consider: what has been breaking us, what is it that we can tame, what wildness can we harness?' – **clare e. potter**

'In Christina Thatcher's vivid new collection, the farm offers wildness and wonder to a young girl, as she witnesses bodies broken and made strong again. *Breaking a Mare* shows us that the breaking can be part of the survival.' – **Rebecca Goss**

Breaking a Mare

Christina Thatcher

PARTHIAN

Parthian, Cardigan SA43 1ED
www.parthianbooks.com
First published in 2025

ISBN 978-1-917140-24-9
Editor: Susie Wildsmith
Cover design by Emily Courdelle
Cover image by Tamara Elnova
Typeset by Elaine Sharples
Proofread by Imogen Davies
Printed and bound by 4edge Limited, UK
Published with the financial support of the Books Council of Wales
British Library Cataloguing in Publication Data
A cataloguing record for this book is available from the British Library
Printed on FSC accredited paper

CONTENTS

Welcome to the Barn

Picture its broom-swept aisle, varnished stalls,
leather saddles, solid silver clasps,
bright unbitten apples, waiting
the row of riding boots, knee-high and oiled.

Again: leather saddles, solid silver clasps,
picture young girls with their braided hair,
the row of riding boots, oiled and quiet,
hens walking in a neat line—

see them: pretty girls braiding their hair,
the mares brushed smooth and shining,
roosters in a row, crowing like they do,
keep going—what can you picture now?

The mares hold their perfect bodies still.
How *good* they are, these bright young girls.
What can you picture now? Just imagine
the varnished stalls with their silver locks.

Show Day

Balancing on a foot stool, boots still
to be polished, the cold of this concrete barn hanging

like a wet sheet around your shoulders, you spread
your arm to measure the mane, estimate

the bulk needed for each braid,
every calculation crowded with worry:

if you don't guess right, if you can't crack
the code of evenness, you will have to start again.

You parse out strands—cross over and under,
pull white-knuckle tight, then cinch. Don't worry

how, later, the mane will catch, how the elastic
will rip out a palm-full of hairs, how the mare

will throw her head, struggle to be still
after a day of trotting, too impatient

for de-braiding. Don't concern yourself, yet,
with cramping hands, worn out from criss-crossing.

For now, this just has to look pretty.
For now, this just has to be perfect.

For protection, calluses rise up

on your hands and feet and you're proud
until you get to school and you're told
that these are *ugly* things   *boy* things
but you can trace them back to the day
you launched hay bales into the loft
the evening hunt for your errant pony
and so you say *no they're not   they're cool*
to a crowd of other children laughing
at what a *farm girl* you are   so you unfurl
your hands like bats until everyone can see
every callus   could come close enough
to pick them clean   but won't   they think
they're *gross*   they think you're *gross*   but
we both know who will win this fight

Get Back on the Horse

It's summer and the flies are back
and your mare is wild-eyed and uneasy
tossing her head as she trots, jolting
as trucks arrive in the driveway, you
keep kicking, you want to canter:
come on girl, let's go and then
she does let you go—

                    her head slung low,
hocks bent, hindquarters taut springs
and too soon you're airborne, too soon
you're crumpled on the ground while
she is bucking, trying to unsaddle herself
and your mom is shouting: *get up!*

You know the rule—never show
you're willing to stay down, never
whimper—just dust yourself off
and jump back in the saddle,
no matter how much your softness
has been bruised, you must *get back on*
and by you, you mean

your mother returning to the trailer,
night after night, where your father waits
in the dark. You don't know which
one of them is the horse, which one
is the saddle. All you know is your duty
to get back on and so you do.

The Good Hose

From a distance it resembles a rough snake:
bright green, yellow stripes running

under its belly. This hose is clear of clogs,
its coating dirt resistant. Even when lugged down

the aisle, heavy with water, it never drips.
One fold near the nozzle keeps everything dry

until it's slipped into a bucket to gush, waterfall,
burst, cascade. No, none of these verbs are right.

Just look—this hose is doing exactly what it promised.

Sweeping Sonnet

here you are again *sweep* pushing the big-bristled broom
down the aisle *sweep* its handle too long *sweep* for your
small girl body at once *sweep* too smooth and splintery *sweep*
the broom walks ahead of you *sweep* like your father
sweep the sound *sweep* its own kind of shushing *sweep*
your two tiny feet following *sweep* the broom parting
the hay *sweep* and dirt *sweep* and chicken shit
sweep you no closer *sweep* to gleaming *sweep*
but still you *sweep* and *sweep* and *sweep*
and *sweep* and *sweep* and *sweep* and
watch and *sweep* and *sweep* the door is arriving
and *sweep* the sun its own kind of praise *sweep*
and push *sweep* more *sweep* *sweep* *sweep*
some things *still* seem earnable

The Man Down the Street

tells you he can talk to animals, is best with geese but speaks sheep and dog and a little cat. He says he's psychic, that the rusted trailer he calls home is just a ruse. If people knew the truth, they'd kill him. But he can tell you because you're special. You love animals too. He pulls wildflowers from his sleeve for you. Says he watches you lead ponies to the barn so sweetly. Hears you call their cute names. Sees your smile, even from a distance. We are so alike, he says, I listen to your parents fighting in the night. You and I both know what this crazy world can do. But it just takes one kind soul to save you. He slips chocolate from his pocket and presents it like an apple to a horse. He knows you will be gentle with his secrets. He reaches out to take your lucky hand.

The Man Marries the Bay Mare

after Patricia Lockwood

The man marries her
            braided tail, four white fetlocks. The man
marries her elegant neck   and   cart-pulling haunches.
The man marries her quiet whinny   her circular head toss.
The man marries the salt on her tongue
                                        her half-broken teeth.

            He marries the moonlight on her withers.

The man marries her pedigree papers.   The man marries
the sawdust stuck to her hooves. He marries each fly
on her flank. He marries her wonky chestnuts and winging gait.
           The man marries her best-fitting bridle and saddle.
                  He marries her stall   and the bolt on its door.

            He marries the air around her body.

He marries every warm exhale.
            The man marries every organ individually.
                  The man marries every hair individually.

The man marries his own hand as he strokes her.
He marries his own tongue,
his thin lips mouthing
                                  that's it, good girl.

Haunted Hayride

He waits in the woods,
clicks his mare's bit against her teeth,
holds her head in place,
          he is silent as a blade.

He stays stiff as the tractor saunters past,
pulling its hay cart of children and parents
holding their breath,
          he must not be seen headless, yet.

The tractor stops. He is about to race
towards it at full speed, his mare geared
to gallop out of darkness, get so, so close—

          they appear and everyone screams

but what is most surprising
is that he is not a *he* at all
          but my mother
dressed as this hallowed legend

          and now look at me,
keeping still on that hay cart,
the only child pretending
to be brave.

Early Morning Shedding Ritual

In the even silence before a child
          cries or husband grumbles, before
                    the snake wakes in his nest, when

the foggy anger from the night before
          evaporates, when the first birds chirp
                    we're alive, we're alive, when

everything she never did returns, circling
          the lipped edge of her mug, she sheds
                    her motherness, her wifeness,

hovering above this ceramic precipice, she exists
          in both her lived life and the one she imagined.
                    Here, in the even silence,

she drinks black coffee until there is nothing left.

My Mother Knits the Matriarchal Home

She is taller than all of us.
Her thighs like great grain barrels,
arms the length of pitchforks. Through
the power of needles, my brother is transformed
into an aqua blue beetle. I am a yellow megaphone.
Our tiny wool father could fit in a change purse,
thin as alfalfa hay. In his left hand: a red cigarette.
Even here, he cannot be completely unarmed. We wait
at her feet as she knits our bedrooms: one pink, one blue.
She stitches a padlock for every door. She unspools
and a farmhouse kitchen appears, the stove and knives
so high only she can reach them. Her purl is perfect.
The master bedroom stays missing. She leaves unstitched
the bed, the bureau, the closeted wedding dress. Instead,
she knits tea kettles—black and blue and purple—each one
larger than the last. She stuffs their bellies with cotton,
sets one on every burner. She lays down her needles
to pray, to plead, to hold her breath and listen,
but none of them can whistle here, nothing
in this place can cry out.

Heard at the Hay Farm

It's all about sound here: the slow rumble
of her Chevy truck over gravel, the quick cut
of an engine, her lungs sucking deep—
grunts and grumbles of a lower key emerging
from her throat—the first language of hay.
Then it's the squeak of the leather seat
as she straightens her spine, thrusts shoulders back,
slaps the steering wheel, the twang of rubber band cinching
her ponytail tighter, the creak of a flipped mirror
to check her cheeks still show dirt. She tells me *be good*,
slams the door and then it's grit being crushed beneath
her stomping shoes, hoof-like and ready to kick
as the baritone choir of hay men rises and falls:
Need a hand sweetheart? Let me help you with that.
Her *nos* and *I'm fines* keep them at bay as she heaves
the shushing hay above her knees, throws each bale
into the banging bed of the truck again and again and again
until it cries like an injured beast. The men's boots shuffle,
their mouths snicker, the quiet money makes its way
to their hands, the mowers and rakes and wrappers
cheer their machine cheers as she leaps into our truck
where my small girl mouth can only whisper *wow*.

No poem, not even this one, can capture her

She is nothing like a ballerina except, perhaps, in her thighs and ankles. She dislikes that mothers are expected to bake. She would bitch-slap Martha Stewart, arm wrestle Joe Biden and hug Judge Judy. She believes dogs can remember their past lives. She plants marigolds in bunches to keep spiders away. Her laugh—like spoons clattering into a barrel—can be heard at the end of the drive. She strokes newborn chicks with the tenderness of a clockmaker. She sleeps well in the presence of geese. Fear has slowed but never stopped her. She can teach horses to bend their necks like perfect crescent moons. When she speaks, everyone listens. When she speaks, everyone gulps. She knows how much blood a colt needs to survive. She keeps a slow cooker under the stairs for guests. Her home is hung with bridles, stained glass and fly traps. When she smiles, everyone smiles back. Her anger is volcanic. Mares come before she calls them. Her body is an imperfect machine. When she loves, you'll know.

The Earth Witch Tells

how the dust never shakes off, even
after stripping, even after climbing
back onto the horse. How mud clumps
in the hair, smears on the cheek. How
everything is *dirty*, how she is always
dirty from heaving shit onto the shit pile.
How when it rains, cliffs crash into creeks
at her bidding. How she anticipates
the turning of her body into mulch,
how she will sink into the earth,
decompose and recompose, then
transform into anything:
a cottonmouth, an oak,
a man, another
girl.

Hide and Seek

after Selima Hill

I followed without fuss.

I thought you were just a boy, the same way
I was just a girl, but I was wrong. I thought
you were calling me to climb the beech trees
with their slender, easy branches. I thought when
you took my hand you were leading me
somewhere comfortable. I did not realise
the moon had already risen.

Before this, I loved the sound of your laugh.

In that moment, your voice was nothing
like a church bell, your skin nothing like mine.
I thought you knew what games I liked to play.
I thought I was fast and strong for a girl but
I was wrong, again. I did not realise my fists
could become egg-like, crack open.

Before this, the forest was fun.

Unearthing

as we laid on that bed   our teenage bodies
naked and still unsexed   he said *this is not*
working out   the other girls gave him more
he needed *encouragement*   moans or whispers
or something   he said *I'm good at this you know*
but I didn't know   and so I stayed quiet unless
something felt really good   and so I stayed quiet
nearly all of the time   and so he asked *what's wrong*
with you   and I guess there must have been
something wrong   then   for me   not to be
the same   as his other girls   moaning
and writhing   like cats on the pavement
what is wrong with me   this eager but dry
uncertainty   unquivering skin   aglow
in the dark   buried coal between my thighs
and his thick hands   just digging and digging
trying to extract it   in this room   a black mine
at midnight   it is only now I realise my body
was not the fuel in this story   but the canary
the snuffed silence   the dead limp of mouth   a saviour.

To him, to him who

reached over and brushed my child thigh
wet from the beach   to him who slipped

his fingers into my first bra while I wasn't
looking   to him who stuffed his hand

down my pants in the classroom where
everyone laughed   to him who reached

into my back pocket in the back of the barn
and squeezed   to him who walked up to us

four quiet girls and unzipped then slapped
his penis on our table just before dinner   to him

who revealed he was a shapeshifter   first snake
then warthog then mole   to him who ate

like a termite   pecked like a woodpecker
to him who was a wolf in disguise   *there is always a wolf*

to him who was a siren   a decoy
yes   your songs fooled me

young as I was

In Praise of Fly Repellent

Remember the satisfaction of sweating,
legs dangling down the barrel of a horse.

Remember the tense clenching of shoulders
whenever breeze flies landed on your mare.
How she quivered but couldn't shake them.

Remember that sharp day in summer,
that one, particular fly. The elation
you felt when you saw it and realised
you were still holding the spray bottle—

hadn't yet handed it to the girl below, so
you could still aim right between its horror eyes.
Remember, in slow motion, pulling the trigger,
watching the jet stream douse its wings, your gaze
following as the fly plummeted down

to the dusty earth, disoriented and bloodless.
That was the first time you saved yourself.
Can you remember what it felt like to escape,
your skin untouched? Doesn't it seem like a dream now—
to remain unhurt, to gallop away
without being chased?

You were carefree, once, but now

whenever you put your foot in the stirrup
and feel your weight drag down the saddle
you worry the girth isn't tight enough or
perhaps it's too tight and your horse might
not be able to breathe or her skin will get caught
as she gallops or that, even, the saddle itself
—say the cinch or the fender or the billet strap—
will get wrapped around a tree and your mare
will be pulled to a stop in the woods and hung.

You worry, too, that as you trot along the trails
your horse will spot a big buck and fear the sharp
wound of its antlers, and then she will take off
tripping and careening into the creek headfirst
and you will be too slow to eject. Perhaps
it's not a deer at all but a bear. Or perhaps
it's just a falling branch that spooks your mare
and you are thrown, your head smashing
like a watermelon against an oak. And then
you imagine fizzing hornets and biting snakes
and hunters' bullets and too fast cars and
bat-filled trees. *And what else? What else*
could there possibly be?

You walk into your kitchen

and tumbling from the fridge is every ear of corn
you've ever eaten, suddenly whole.

Pick up the closest cob, *that one*, grab it
from the Thanksgiving when you were eight,

when everyone was still alive and your thin
uncle gave you a present: plastic cob holders

in the shape of little corns. It was the first time
you had your own sharp object to take home.

It was the first kernel of understanding,
the very moment you realised that a big thing

can be eaten by a smaller version of itself.
You stopped talking as everyone ate, pushed

with all the push a child has those two tiny prongs
into the corn, and understood, then, the pleasure

of that pushing, the delight that one can get
from control. Later, you stashed those holders

somewhere secret, knew you would need them
to stop the hunger in your house.

Listen Here, Girl

be grateful for the roof over your
head for the big window be
grateful for the back door
buzzing fridge be grateful for the
milk the table the food a
dishwasher be grateful for the
radio in your room be grateful
for the wood stove dogs cats and
horses more grateful for your
legs your teacher teaching you be
grateful for it be grateful he
doesn't drink like he did be
grateful for anyone who gives
you a job be grateful for work be
grateful your car still drives be
grateful when any man looks
your way be grateful for the quiet
be grateful for chirping birds be
grateful for shoes and coats for
the cold be grateful for the
willow and the creek be grateful
that rich boy even noticed you
be grateful your body is so
touchable be grateful you had
somewhere to run back to

Breaking a Mare

Early dawn, your body abuzz,
your mind hawk alert, you slide
into the barn and act as though
nothing is different.

This is not the day you will break her.

In a cartoon, this is the moment
the wolf would start whistling,
twiddling his thumbs: *no one*
will be eaten today.

You approach her stall, glide on
the eager bridle, lead her to the centre
aisle where you lean until she remembers
your weight.

You whistle as you wrap
the saddle around her back,
        her eyes remain tame
even as you walk together
to the stream-side paddock where

you guide her body to the wall—
nothing to see here—then slip
your foot in the stirrup, make
the leap,

            her eyes shift

what happens next

is a poem.

It Happened in Slow Motion

The horse rearing up like a stilt walker

Her tumbling off like a weakened acrobat

The horse falling back like a great oak, chopped down

Her lungs deflating like a whoopee cushion

Her ribs folding like deck chairs

Her eyes like glittering fishhooks

Your little legs, like something fast you can't think of now

running to the phone in the house

and then back

to the ring like a capsized boat

Her body, a wet pile of clothes

The ambulance like a lighthouse foghorn

The hospital like a cave, echoing

with her like the

and you like a

For all this filly knew, my mother was a mountain lion

on her back and she poor girl the prey the claws of fear too much
to bear bucking the first answer then rearing and kicking while
my mother reached round her neck trying to control and calm
in equal measure this girl Beamer light of the pasture
hot as a hornet and fast how quick she learned
to succumb ears jerked to my mother's voice
eyes like trapped fish she did not realise
her own unbrokenness until she felt this
mighty weight on her body another
unwanted body until she could not
get it off until she sweating and
stamping and twisting
had no choice but to
let her self
break

Private Lesson Ghazal

Do it again. Settle your spine and find your seat,
your bones should never sit hard on the seat

but move like fluid cursive, converting messages
from your body to your horse's body, your seat

must not speed up or slow down, otherwise your horse
will follow. Listen. The equine back is sensitive, loose seats

encourage slack, an unwelcome sway and swing.
Remember, this is about control. Your seat

must lead and follow your horse, never jackhammer
or pop. Stop. Focus now. You can strengthen your seat

by imagining an invisible string running from heel,
to pelvis, to shoulder, to head. Don't let your seat

get lazy. You got that? Relax your lower back
and sit deep until you secure your seat

in the centre of this horse, in the centre
of this ring—girl, always remember your place.

She never steeples her hands

instead she prays with her pitchfork
bends at the knees lifts hot from cold
snaps up turns to the wheelbarrow she moves
from left to right the way you read this scraping
and sifting lifting and dumping until everything
is clean again every stall every morning is emptied
and re-bedded she walks with the grace of a pastor
through the barn she knows it will be dirty again tomorrow
she knows the hay bales will split and the grain will spill
and the creek will freeze then flood and shit will keep dropping
and the kids will cut their hands and the brood mare will colic
and someone will get kicked and the fences will need mending
and the hose will run out of water and the gravel man won't arrive again
and the rats will come back and she will need to inject the weakened colt
and her own children will never understand her and the stallion's roof will
crumble and there won't be enough money to feed herself and she will
collapse her lungs again and she will die here eventually she will
die here and this is why she yells to anyone who will listen
there's work to be done, come on!

The Barn Gives Counsel to All Women Who Enter

Grind yourself, feel the weight of each hay bale,
every wire scratch a mark of progress. *Keep going*
even when that man calls you from the stairs,
even when that child plays alone in the corner,
even when your body has crumbled like clay.

Grind yourself, work until your skin wears
so thin over your bones that you become translucent
until, one day, you can lay in your farmhouse bed
without guilt, a reach away from the shotgun
that released so many mares.

Grind yourself, until there is nothing left
and the dust of you can be swept under the earth.
This time must be spent somehow. *Never be still.*
The best horses know how to whip themselves.
The best women know how to work.

Here We Are

— women in my family take punches
throw them   eat apples with too few teeth
tame horses and dogs   drink milk jug cider
cry quiet so their children can't hear

— women in my family stand taller
than they are   curse and spit first
then say sweet things until
every door is locked

— women in my family survive
the birth room   usually   scream
like ambulance sirens   nurse welts
with frozen fruit   wounds with meat

— women in my family *push, hold, stay*
even after   their bodies attack them
even after   their bodies are attacked
even after   they give themselves up

Not Our Fight

I was seated, you were standing, flitting first between stove and sink, then fridge and whiskey glass. I was seated and you were pacing, your arms flung up like fly swatters. I was seated and you stopped, pressed your back against the sink, eyes like a fox darting between me, the floor, me again, the stove. I was seated, my voice standing up before me. I did not recognise the sound. I was seated, you were throwing your hands up and then clamping them onto your hips. I was seated but not anymore. I was standing and you were standing, arms crossed, teeth bright. We were standing and our words boxed between us: *BANG, POW, KAZOW!* Neither one of us backed down, even when we both became too loud. We were standing until we realised our words were not meant for each other. Until we saw, too late, the strings. Our limbs pulled high by ghosts. Our mouths worked wide by ghosts.

Some Say

after Natalie Shapero

Some say foxes' screams drive women mad. Some say
the women were mad to begin with: *What sane woman would run*
into the woods towards a scream? Some say women can't help themselves,
can't quiet their instinct to quiet the screams. Some say women know
these screams are testing them: *foxes cry like human babies*. Some say
foxes are helpless too. Some say foxes know what they're doing,
conniving little things. Some say madness is the very best place,
that when women reach it they stop hearing. Some say
the screams were never from foxes at all.
Some say every scream is an echo.

Sudden Blacksmith

So what you gonna do girl?
These blades need to be sharp
and I mean fucking sharp
to get this done. Chop chop,
or your poor lame pony
won't be able to stand.
Come on. Quick!
This pony's in pain—
look at her buckled knees,
her crumbling hooves. Stay still.
Your hands are jumping.
STOP. Start again.
Your pony needs you. Wait,
don't do that. You don't know
what you're doing.
Your nippers have gone
haywire now. Keep steady
for Christ's sake!
Don't you love your pony?
Don't you want to save her?
Careful, you're sweating.
That'll ruin the blade.

The Knife Orchard

The sign outside the gate reads: *cover yourself.*
Puncture-proof robes are free at the entrance.
Women obey, used to these instructions, but

men scoff. Some strip and stride inside.
Some run in, war-crying. Every wound a badge
of strength. The more bleeding the better.

The orchard grower knows how to bait.
I bet you can't make it through without crying.
Wives beg their husbands to cover up.

But, no, these men have practiced
puncturing for months, mastered zigzagging.
This is their test and they are ready.

Some women hold signs at the exit: *I believe in you!*
Some talk about their men in high, pleasant voices.
Others sigh, wait in their cars. A few enter

the orchard themselves. Bleeding men duck
and dive and run but these robed women just walk,
calm as silt. The knives glisten, wave hello.

Redneck Ecologies

pine trees pile in, a property line marked

with beer cans, plastic toys, shotgun shells

vegetable patches ringed with electric wire

bear traps gape, the ground compacts

under half-ton pickups, engine oil seeps

into soil, the geese wade through mud

necks too short to snatch grass

beyond chain-link

chickens leave their coop for little seed

cluck wild when the house screams

the old pony whinnies from her stall and,

nightly, the neighbour's wolfdog howls

at the lone streetlamp

Bilocation

what I am writing carries me back to the sound of my mother's voice: her *whistle, air kiss, cheek click*, hollering *time to come in girls, let's go!* The mares' heads raising from the turning grasses, their hooves swift towards the grain. We all hear it: the bright bang of metal on metal, the sloshing bucket waiting for them, half full and not yet turning to ice. Here / there the clouds are lowering in autumn. Goosebumps lift from my skin even now; these fresh-coated horses, so close to the surface, trotting to the barn for dinner. These oaks are starting to tip their fat leaves to the ground. Soon we'll be able to see the newly built houses encroaching our treeline, the golf course outcropping our cornfield. Like a child peeking through her fingers, soon, we'll look down the drive and see two roads which lead *away*. Winter unpeels trees and exposes us: there is a world beyond the barn and what are we to do with it?

Convincing a Horse to Cross the Tohickon Bridge

She knows stepping off the edge
of a cliff is unnatural, that hooves do not belong

on iron. She knows catching glimpses of river beneath
our bellies is abnormal. She knows she is not meant

to move from this place to *that* place. She knows she should listen
to the earth, take the safest route. She knows the bridge

is green but not the *right* kind of green. She knows she shouldn't
have a rider, even, shouldn't have to bite metal. She knows

she is not meant to be here, standing at the brink
of this bridge, but what should she do? What *can* she do, now?

How sad the creek was

when the girl drowned, no one could see it
because the creek is always wet but she was *very* sad.
It is her nature to be wet, it is her nature to bulge
with rain, it is her nature to be swift, her rapids
rushing the rocks and yet it is not natural
to rise this high, to drown people, and certainly not her,
this little girl who was swept up, unsteady
from the edge. If only the creek had arms,
if only she had the power to slow and go dry,
offer this girl a safe place to stand.
The creek can do other things, sure.
She gives home to the smallmouth bass.
She gives water to the waterfowl.
She gives root to the alder shrubs on her banks.
The dogwood blooms, thanks to her, and yet
she cannot forget this girl. If only the creek
were different but she isn't, she wasn't, and now
miles away, upstream, there is a funeral
happening and the creek has no good mouth
to say *I'm sorry.*

When it's time, she sounds

nothing like an owl, nothing
like the lowest note of a trumpet.
You can't compare her to swishes
of taffeta or the crack of confetti canons.
She could never be mistaken for
the hush of a slow stream.
There is nothing
that sounds quite like a ginkgo
in the forest, in October, releasing
her stinking fruit like a Changuan robe,
nothing like that faint *pfft*
as her flesh and seeds separate, hit
the woodland floor with no him
to hear for miles and miles.

Sawdust Carousel

Round and round, the men heave
trunks onto trucks, hulk branches

onto backs. Conveyer belts spin
with the promise of a new season.

The mill plumes for miles, sweet sap
evaporates in sawing. Our arrival

is the smell of pine, the sensation
of a sneeze rising, thousands of trees

now skin soft. The brood mares
need this bedding, an echo of forests,

a balm for ache. We shovel shavings
into our pickup as the men swing their axes,

wonder how many chops it will take
to break their wooden hearts.

When the Knacker Man Visits the Barn

he's polite, says *please bear with me*
as he heaves our dead pony onto his cart.

He doesn't mind picking out bullets, setting
cracked knees, getting blood on his white cottons.

His aim is to make the dead look good as they depart.
He wants them to go naturally.

As he leaves, we see our pony's eyes shining
like rock pools, her hooves tucked neatly away.

We shout *goodbye!* and no one retches. We shout *goodbye!*
and remind ourselves that death is not the end for her.

We know that ponies can do anything, can become
anything: a lily, a leather jacket, a new book,

a sleek and carnivorous mink.

The Race

Okay, yes, we know they won't win,
these wild horses racing our black truck
as we *vroom* towards mountains.
We know they can't outrun us, but
perhaps we could slow down, offer victory
like we do for our kitten, pretending
as she leaps – claws out – onto our wrists
that she is strong enough to defeat us.
We must let her win sometimes
otherwise she'll become depressed, and then joy
will be sucked from our house. So, we pull over,
watch the mares *zoom* away
so much faster than we imagined, so much
faster than our own legs can run. And yes,
we see it now as they top the ridge, tails flying.
We see how wrong we have been.

Mapping a Horse

How easily grey areas can hide
beneath the barrel, the hair
an uncharted terrain, the slope
of neck like a mountain struggling
to rise. How wave-like the crest
of a wither, the pine needle prick
of ear tips. How simply manes
can deceive, shaken like summer
grasses. How the sand dune roll
of shoulders awes us, muzzles
softer than our own skin.
                                        How we find
ourselves swiftly unmade in this land,
how we can never see beyond it.

Quarter Horse Elegy

for Chance

                                        Just one ride
and lovestruck quick for all of it:
your muscled shoulders stretched
beneath me like a perfect machine,
your mane thousands of tiny kites
in the sweet wind, the suction sound
of mud in hooves as we rode through
feathery grasses then entered the woods
where I grew into me as you slowly
disappeared underneath.

It took ____ to get here

to the field
where Mamma
Mare was shot
just out of eye's reach
from the barn, just after
she kicked the concrete wall
her leg dangling, sinews
like frayed electric wire,
my own mother's wail
hitting the tin roof
like thunder
even the chickens
stopped *cawing.*

She must still be here
somewhere.

I don't recall
the name of her dead foal,
grief powering that last
unbearable kick,
but can still hear
my father riding her
through the woods, his
good girl firecracker come on now enough—

the ground is rocky here.

How far could her body
have been dragged? Help me
scour this field for her bones.

The Next Stage

Before her bones are hoisted from dirt
give her a new name, her own. Rope off
space so she can reassemble in peace.
Keep her a safe distance from stallions.
Give her the good grass, don't worry
over fatty grains—health is important
but so is decadence. Pair her with other mares.
Notice how her ears perk up—her hooves
don't crack. She is rarely grumpy now.
Teach her cutting, barrel racing, roping, even
dressage. Her whinny is a parade trumpet,
her teat an untouched jewel. Let her live
on the top-aisle, forget her old stall
beside all the foals and fillies crammed
with their mothers. Let the purring cats
in to see her. Look how young and
strong she is now. Her bones will
age nicely. She has the luxury of days.
The shotgun sits quiet in its case.

We played dead

for hours in high stacks of straw, waiting to be found
kept our breath as still as possible, channelled chickens

brought stiff by dogs to the porch, practiced letting go
of our limbs, de-fluttering our eyes, willed our hearts to slow

enough so even we could not hear their jiffy, their pulse
for hours, I was the coffin-clutcher, you the discoverer,

the one who stumbled upon the dead girl—
how skilled you were at *shock*, a gasp like a can of Coke

cracked open, how you lunged straight to the body,
your ear hovering above my mouth, waiting for a slip

of breath, how you grabbed the hay in despair every time
I stayed still long enough to fool you, how after every game

we studied the rat-eaten rabbits to mimic, how
we watched the vet rush in with his gloves to rescue

every colicking mare, how we came to learn
that none of us can ever really be saved.

The Rescue Act

The curtain lifts to a colicking horse:

the audience knows it's colicking because it's laying down,
pointing its muzzle to its belly

The horse cannot throw up. The horse cannot sweat enough
to save itself. All it can do is roll for relief.

A woman runs on stage, shouts: Get up! Get up! Bad horse!
The woman brings a crop to hit with but, still, the horse rolls and rolls.

the audience knows if the horse keeps rolling
its intestines will tie themselves in knots and then
its stomach will burst and its blood will flood
with tiny bits of grain that it never should have eaten
in the first place and, then, it will die

the audience assumes that the horse
wants to be comfortable again
wants to be unafraid
wants to be cooed at, unwhipped

The woman keeps yelling and yelling.
the audience starts to boo and hiss and stamp their feet
The woman grips the crop harder, whips faster.

Eventually, the horse stops rolling. Both the woman and the horse wait.
Eventually, the horse stands. Eventually, the horse walks.

Both the woman and the horse make noises which sound like sighs of relief.
Both the woman and the horse take a bow.

In this universe, the dogs

from *Where the Red Fern Grows* stay alive:
the mountain lion never arrives to gut
Old Dan, Little Ann never dies from grief
at his grave, the red fern never grows. Instead,
Billy and his Redbone Coonhounds traverse
the Ozarks, cross four states to find me
under my bedroom blanket, praying for them
to survive, and then, suddenly, they arrive,
tap tap on my window, mouthing *come with us*
and, because this is all my young self ever prayed for,
I follow them to the back meadow, past the rotting
car and broken sofa, past dogwood trees
and duck ponds, past the quarry and hospital,
past empty fields and playgrounds, through
the doors of my elementary school and
into the reading room where all the other children
have gathered, books open, to weep.

Reanimation

after Sean Shearer

Black. Less black. The flicker
of long eyelashes. Blood dribbles back
to the bullet hole in the white blaze
of her face. Nostrils flare to the size
of tiny apples. A snort and her eyes roll
open. The cannon bone knits itself
back together. Muscles twitch.
Her foreleg slips underneath her shoulder,
bears weight. The other follows, then
the hind legs bring up the rear.
Her knees lock into place. The heft
of her body is held up. She lifts
her head, hears my whistle, my call:
Dusty, come here girl, come on!
She gallops towards my voice, the field
greener than it's ever been.

Bonds

In the space between bit and rein,
between hand and hoof, silence
hangs. At any moment

trees can turn skeletal, pupils can dilate,
unease can ripple beneath withers
and skin, show us how breath

can turn to wings in our bodies,
how trust can unspool two
natural things.

The First Lady of Rodeo

for Tad Lucas

You never see the crowd: in photos
their faces blur, so the foreground is just her teeth,
her mouth always open, exalting. She is *so good*
at this and she knows it. Her famous fringed
chaps focus her lassoing body, always,

she holds one rein tight, lifts the other hand to wave,
to find rhythm, to ride hard her tired animal. *How does she do it?*
How does she beam? Her lipstick never smudged,
her shirt always buttoned, yet she moves

quick as a tadpole, slides from the top of her saddle to the belly
of a galloping bronco, then swings back, stands
as the horse runs and runs, perfectly balanced,
her back arched, arms up, her face
a reflection of the sun.

The Female Rodeo Clown

must protect the rider, lure the bucking bull
from every injured man. When the crowd
needs distracting from blood and bone,
she must crack jokes, start singalongs,
tear off her own clothes.

When the bull returns, she must be savvy,
map its movements: *spinning, sunfishing, breaking*
in two. When the rider jumps to save himself
she'll whip off her bra to wave in the air:
yoo hoo, come and get me!

The bull cannot resist so, as the cowboy shuffles
to safety, the clown leaps in her body-sized barrel,
braces herself for the beast to kick. She prays
horns cannot pierce sheet metal, hopes
her greasepaint is not running in the heat.

The Rodeo Paradox

for Mabel Strickland Woodward

She could rope a steer in 18 seconds,
throw its calf-body to the ground and pin
its flailing legs. Her own calves squeezed magic
into broncos, her forward fenders pulled *oohs*
from the crowd, her one-foot-drag dropped jaws.
This *lovely lady of rodeo* could buck any catcall,
mount any animal—ride unnervingly fast, with grace.
Her brave was the size of a Dallas arena. And yet
she was never *brutish*, reporters rallied around her
petite frame. Even on the night she swung under
her horse's neck, reached up for her saddle,
then slipped—trampled to *near death*—
the papers prized how pretty she looked,
even then, *just so darn beautiful.*

The Rodeo Queen

pretties for pageants first speaks
to her people in the language of sequence

long-flowing hair pink lipstick
she knows the rules the same rules

every woman knows but her reward is bigger
a kingdom an arena a stage

where she cascades in opens the rodeo
perfectly formed her horse an extension

of her body she keeps strong enough to hoist
the flag gallops fast enough for it to wave

the crowd cheers the crowd whistles
the crowd agrees she is a *good girl*

a good American girl by the grace of God
she slows and is safe waves blows kisses

mouths *thank you* to the crowd
thank you *thank you*

the crowd follows her out to the streets
flashes their cameras

she keeps smiling how could they know
what this has taken from her

the open wound of her mirror
the deep cave of her barn

The Rodeo Tragedy

for Bonnie McCarroll

The crowd was not ready for her immodest pain.
Suffering should never be invited by pretty girls, in public.

    In public, pretty girls should be predictable.
    The girl was tenderly gathered up and hastily removed to hospital.

Calling her a girl is a lie—Bonnie was about to retire.
Black Cat was an *honest* bronc, he was just *agitated* that day.

    Agitated, the gate jumped open and pretty Bonnie rode strong.
    Black Cat turned a sudden somersault. We know the rest.

We know the rest: Death was too slow for comfort.
The crowd saw too much of trampled, pretty Bonnie.

    Some believe Bonnie was a bronc in another life.
    What a relief it would be for her prettiness to mean nothing.

Cowboys still believe that cowgirls are breakable.
The crowd was not ready for her immodest pain.

First Time

for my grandmother, Jeanne E. Stein

How did it feel? Newly woman,
only one in that dusty ring,
the bronc smashing
his gate, side-lined men
hollering, all of this
before the quiet orbit
of my grandfather,
of my mother, of me,
but even then, you must
have known yourself:
there you were
ready to ride,
feet glued to stirrups
free hand electric,
what happened to
your heart when that gate
was unlocked, the heave
of that tsunami
horse beneath you,

your spurs flying up

his muscular shoulders,

did the crowd go silent

behind you, hold

their breath

for the full eight

seconds, or could you

hear every cheer—

adrenaline does

funny things

to the body—

and what happened

in the end,

were you thrown

to the ground,

did you slide down

the saddle, limp

twisted away, or—

in front of everyone,

suddenly—

did you win?

Interweaving

On a bus, hurtling from one town to another,
a woman braids her hair, an apple's breadth

from the rattling window where road and
farmland meet. How strange to see this here,

after so many years: my mother's mane
in this faraway place—her flyaways breaking

loose, her split end static darting faster
than spooked sheep. How strange this electric

urge to release my own locks from their stale
ponytail and mimic these braids:

the same weave as these horses,
the same soft as these women.

Keeper

Bring the apples, the sweet grains,
the rope. Bring the spurs, the saddle

opened like a ribcage. Bring the whip,
the unsaid carried on your shoulders

like a cloak. Bring your heart splashing
like a river. Bring the belief that there is

only one god who can save, even though
every horse knows there are many.

Bring your fear like its own soft prayer.
Bring your two ripe ears and, finally, listen.

Glossary

Breaking: the process of training a horse to be ridden. Horses progress from being *unbroken*, with no experience of being handled or carrying weight; to *halter/bridle/saddle broke*, when they become accustomed to riding equipment; then to *dumb broke*, when they're able to follow basic commands; and, finally, to *well broke* or *broke to death*, when they're comfortable being ridden, responsive to commands and suitable for riders of any skill level.

Bronc: an unbroken horse used in bronc riding events at rodeos. These horses habitually buck, i.e. jump into the air and kick out their back legs; rear up, i.e. 'stand' on their hind legs with their forelegs off the ground; and spin, or otherwise move unpredictably, in order to throw the rider off their back.

Bull: an uncastrated male cow used for bull-riding events at rodeos. Bulls are more powerful than broncs and move differently. Bulls are known for their 'belly roll' or 'sunfishing', when their bodies are completely off the ground and their feet are kicking to the side in a twisting, rolling motion. Bulls often spin in tight, quick circles and can, sometimes, run or jump extremely high, known as 'breaking in two'.

Colic: a symptom of abdominal pain, colic is one of the most common causes of death in horses. When a horse is *colicking* it means they are exhibiting signs of colic, such as pawing the ground, biting or kicking their belly, lying down or rolling. Colic is often unpreventable.

Filly: a young female horse, usually less than four years old. The word *filly* can also be applied to a girl or young woman, especially if she is lively or spirited. Some scholars believe the word *filly* originated from the Old Norse word *fylja* which means *to follow*.

Haunted Hayride: a Halloween event where a group of people sit in an open trailer—normally used for hay—and are towed by a tractor through a wooded area. These hayrides usually happen at night and feature actors portraying serial killers, monsters, ghosts and other frightening figures. Some hayrides may even include special effects or recognisable characters like Frankenstein, Freddy Krueger or the Headless Horseman.

Mare: a female adult horse. The word *mare* can also be used when talking to or about a woman in a disrespectful way (i.e. *Stupid mare!)* or to describe a task or experience that is particularly frustrating, difficult or unpleasant (i.e. *Getting here was a real mare!*). A *broodmare* is a female horse kept specifically for breeding.

Rodeo: a competitive equestrian sport which grew out of the working practices of Spanish-Mexican *vaqueros* and 19th-century American cowboys. Rodeos include events such as bronc riding, bull riding, steer wrestling and barrel racing. Rides are often completed in six or eight second intervals—the rider who can stay on the longest without touching their animal, equipment or themself with their freehand, wins. In the USA, professional rodeos are governed and sanctioned by specific associations, although many local and amateur rodeos still operate across the country.

Rodeo Clown: a person whose job it is to distract or 'fight' the bull. Bull-riders may be thrown to the ground and be too disoriented or injured to get out of the arena; it is the rodeo clown's job to attract the bull's attention so the rider can safely escape. Rodeo clowns also provide entertainment during and between rodeo events. Nearly all rodeo clowns are men.

Notes

'The Good Hose' was loosely inspired by Denise Levertov's poem 'The Fountain' from *Poems of Denise Levertov, 1960-1967* (New Directions, 1984).

'The Man Marries the Bay Mare' was written after Patricia Lockwood's poem 'He Marries the Stuffed Owl Exhibit at the Indiana Welcome Center' from *Motherland Fatherland Homelandsexuals* (Penguin, 2017). It is worth noting that I read this collection alongside Lockwood's memoir, *Priestdaddy* (Penguin, 2018) which did not directly inspire this poem but, rather, sparked a wider consideration of confessionalism, poetic ethics, family dynamics and 'dark' work.

'Hide and Seek' was written after Selima Hill's poem 'Modest Acts of Extreme Slowness' from *People Who Like Meatballs* (Bloodaxe, 2012).

'To him, to him who' was inspired by a pottery fragment that poet Clare Shaw found while mudlarking. They shared this fragment, which included the words 'To him, to him who', during a 'January Writing Hours' session on Zoom. This piece also borrows the phrase in italics (*there is always a wolf*) from Fiona Benson's poem 'Red Riding Hood', published in her collection *Ephemeron* (Jonathan Cape, 2022).

'Listen Here, Girl' would probably not exist if I had never read José Olivarez's poem 'I Walk Into Every Room and Yell Where the Mexicans At' from *Citizen Illegal* (Haymarket Books, 2018).

'Breaking a Mare' was radically revised after reading John Okrent's 'Ars Poetica on Ice' in *The Poetry Review* (Vol 112, No 3, Autumn 2022). An epiphany moment.

'She never steeples her hands' would probably not exist if I had not read '"Find Work"' by Rhina P. Espaillat from *Poetry* (February, 1999) and had not returned, later in life, to Seamus Heaney's 'Digging' from *Death of a Naturalist* (Faber & Faber, 1966).

'Here We Are''s punctuation—particularly the em dashes on the left-alignment—was inspired by Guinevere Clark's poem 'Ma' from her PhD thesis entitled *The Egg in the Triangle: Poetics of Motherhood, Sexuality and Place*.

'Some Say' was written after Natalie Shapero's poem 'Sunshower' from *Poetry* (November, 2017).

'When the Knacker Man Visits the Barn' has a tricky title because 'knacker man' is a UK term and the half-imagined farm in this poem is located in the USA. According to *A Dictionary of Agriculture and Land Management* (Manley et al, 2019) a knacker man is 'someone who collects dead or dying farm animals, including horses. The animals, unfit for human consumption, are taken to the knacker's yard, where they are cut up into individual parts for further use; for example, the hide might be used for leather.' Also, years and years ago, I was introduced to Toi Derricotte's poem, 'The Minks', published in *Captivity* (University of Pittsburgh Press, 1989). Derricotte's piece—and its ability to investigate wildness, death and transformation—undoubtedly underpins my poem. Her raw-horse-meat-eating minks were just waiting to emerge here.

'Mapping a Horse' (as well as 'Bonds' and 'Keeper') were written in response to Julie Sleaford's moving photography project *The Problem Horse & Other Stories* (2022). I had the privilege of spending months with these photographs, before they were published, and enjoyed several thought-provoking conversations with Sleaford about her photography practice as well as her relationship to horses, mortality, womanhood and more. In addition to inspiring these three poems, Sleaford's photographs and processes influenced my own thinking and poetic approach.

'In this universe, the dogs' is dedicated to anyone who, like me, was broken by Wilson Rawls' novel *Where the Red Fern Grows* (Doubleday, 1961).

'Reanimation' was written after Sean Shearer's poem 'Rewinding an Overdose on a Projector' from *Red Lemons* (University of Akron Press, 2021).

'The First Lady of Rodeo' was written in response to a famous photograph called 'Tad Lucas Riding Hell Cat' (Doubleday, 1945) which is available in the digital archives of the National Cowboy & Western Heritage Museum.

'The Rodeo Paradox' borrows each italic phrase from a newspaper report, blog or website feature written about the famous cowgirl, Mabel Strickland Woodward.

'The Rodeo Tragedy' was written for Bonnie McCarroll, a champion bronc rider whose fatal accident in 1929 led to women being banned from competing in bronc riding events across America. The poem borrows its first italic line (*The girl was tenderly gathered up and hastily removed to hospital*) from Cain Allen's 2005 Oregon Historical Society entry on Bonnie McCarroll. The two other italic words (*honest* and *agitated*) were lifted from Juni Fisher's 2011 article 'The Last Ride of Bonnie McCarroll' where former rodeo clown, Monk Carden—who was near Bonnie as she mounted the bronc, Black Cat—recounts what happened between them.

Acknowledgements

Thanks are due to the editors who first published poems from this collection in the following magazines: *Ambit, Amsterdam Quarterly, Butcher's Dog, Okay Donkey, New Welsh Reader, Poetry Wales, The North, The Poetry Review* and *Under the Radar.*

Gratitude is also due to the editors who published poems from this collection as part of academic texts, anthologies and other artistic projects:

'When it's time, she sounds' was displayed as part of *The Ministry of Environmental Disasters* exhibition (Being Human Festival, Guildford, November 2024).

'When the Knacker Man Visits the Barn' was selected by Paul Muldoon for the '2024 Poems on the Buses Exhibition' in Guernsey.

'Sweeping Sonnet' was longlisted for the 2023 National Poetry Competition.

'How sad the creek was' and 'When it's time, she sounds' were published as part of an academic essay in *Poetry and the Global Climate Crisis: Educational Creative Approaches to Complex Challenges* (Routledge, 2023)

'The Female Rodeo Clown' and 'The Rodeo Queen' were published as part of an academic book chapter in *Intersections of Sport and Society in Creative Writing* (Springer, 2023)

'The First Lady of Rodeo' and 'The Rodeo Paradox' were published as part of an academic article entitled 'Cowgirl Poetics: Writing women in rodeo' in Special Issue 67 of *TEXT* (2022)

'The Race' was published in *Footprints: an anthology of new ecopoetry* (Broken Sleep Books, 2022)

'Mapping a Horse', 'Bonds' and 'Keeper' were written in response to Julie Sleaford's photography project *The Problem Horse & Other Stories* (2022). Sleaford selected one poem, 'Mapping a Horse', to be printed on a postcard which accompanies the photobook.

'Interweaving' was translated into Welsh by Sian Northey and published, in both languages, in the *A470* anthology (Arachne Press, 2022)

'Some Say' was selected by Jacqueline Saphra to be published in *The Ver Prize 2020*, the Ver Poets Open Competition anthology

I am very grateful for the award of a Literature Wales Writer's Bursary, supported by the National Lottery through Arts Council of Wales, for the purpose of researching and drafting the early poems in this collection. Literature Wales' belief in this work came at a pivotal time in my writing career and led me all across the Gower peninsula to track its wild ponies.

I am indebted to the following groups who regularly wrote and workshopped with me over the years: Inksplott, NaPoWriMo Sunday Poetry Kitchen, Dialect Writers Group and the #57 Collective.

Thanks also to the friends and fellow writers who read early drafts of these poems: Heidi Beck, Laurie Bolger, Zillah Bowes, Claire Collison, Emily Cotterill, Rebecca Goss, Julie Elizabeth Griffiths, Paul Henry, Ryan Kuether, JLM Morton, Kate North, Emily Harris, Caleb Parkin, Katherine Stansfield, Hilary Watson and Alice Willitts.

A special thanks to Ailbhe Darcy and Abigail Parry for the pep talks and pub nights. Your generous company steadied me when I really needed it. I am also grateful to my editor, Susie Wild, for believing in this collection and giving it a home at Parthian Books.

I was lucky enough to have worked on this manuscript in some beautiful, quiet places, including The Clockhouse (Arvon), Gladstone's Library and the Tŷ Newydd Writing Centre. My Aunt Karon's kitchen table also provided a welcome space for poem-making.

Gratitude is owed to other family members as well, including my in-laws, Trish and Richard Daly Sr., for their support and subscriptions to poetry magazines; my grandfather, William Stein, for telling me stories about my grandmother's bronc riding days; my brother, Timothy Thatcher, for his endless love and encouragement; my mother, Jessica Stein—who is one of the strongest women I know—for introducing me to the barn, teaching me to ride horses, accepting that I was not very good at riding, and encouraging my poetry.

Finally, endless love is owed to my husband, Richard Daly, who has patiently listened to me read every poem in this collection aloud and who reads poems back to me too, my own and others, when his soothing voice is called for. Thank you, Rich, for our countless conversations, for all the tea, for loving me, for everything.

PARTHIAN *Poetry*

Little Universe

Natalie Ann Holborow

ISBN 978-1-917140-21-8

£10.00 | Paperback

'This is intimate, poignant writing. Stunning imagery bursts from these pages as the speaker's selves open to their surroundings, the reader joining a chorus of "startled applause".'
– John McCullough

Lives bustle within a busy hospital's walls, humming against the Gower landscape that stretches beyond its windows. The tiny worlds of a wide cast unfold as they deal with their own emergencies, losses, recoveries, hopes and histories.

This Common Uncommon

Rae Howells

ISBN 978-1-914595-90-5

£10.00 | Paperback

'Finely wrought, intelligent, and full of heart... an important book that speaks for nature, land, and species which, too often, we see as silent: a vital tome at a time of urgency.'
– Mab Jones, *Buzz Magazine*

When a local common is threatened with development, one poet explores its secrets, discovering extraordinary natural treasures and wonderful people fighting to defend them. Can they save this uncommon common?